NATIONAL GEOGRAPHIC

What Do You Know About Dolphins?

Harley Chan

T0052331

Dolphins swim in the sea.
What do you know about dolphins?

Do you know how a dolphin breathes?

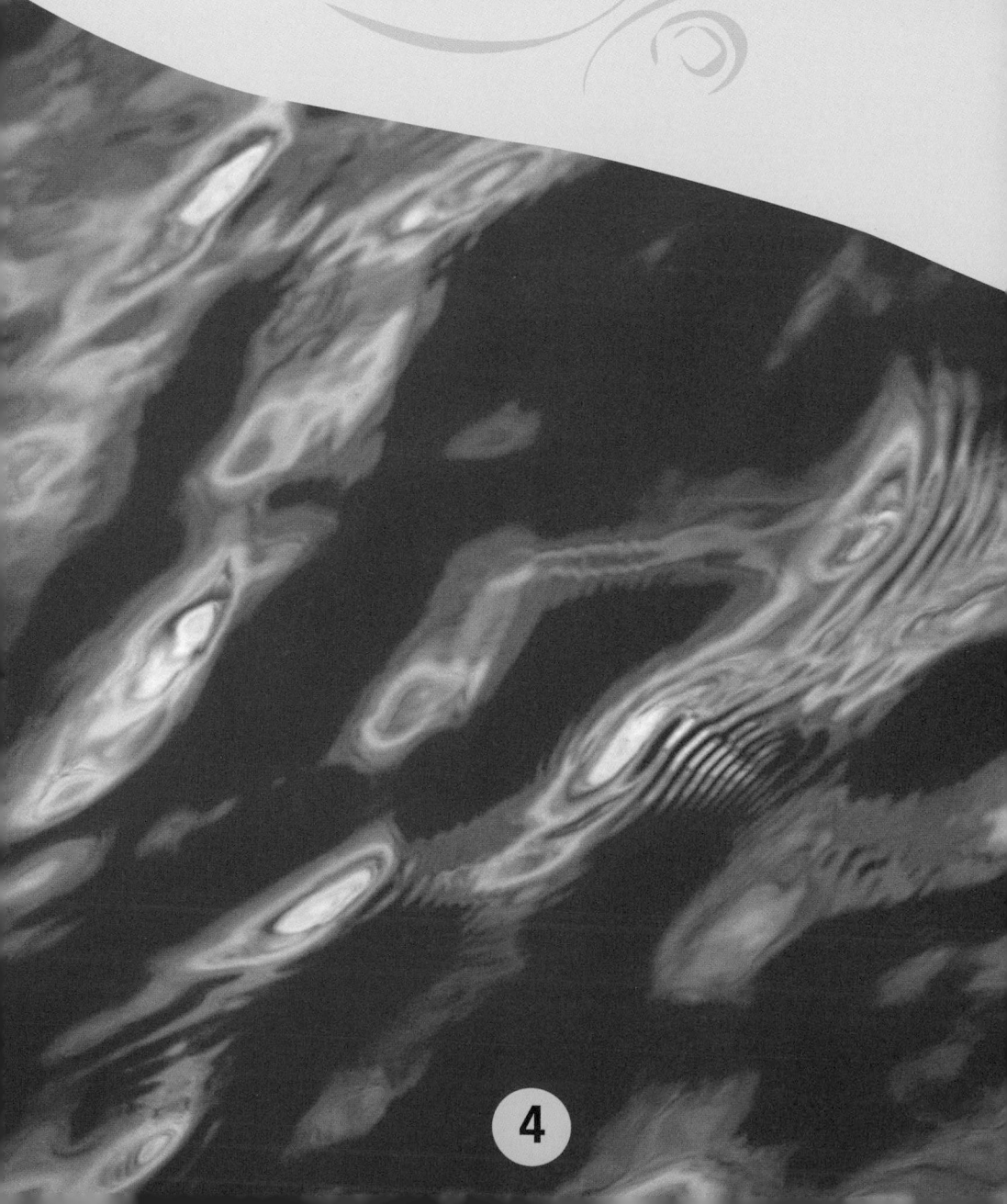

Do you know how a dolphin eats?

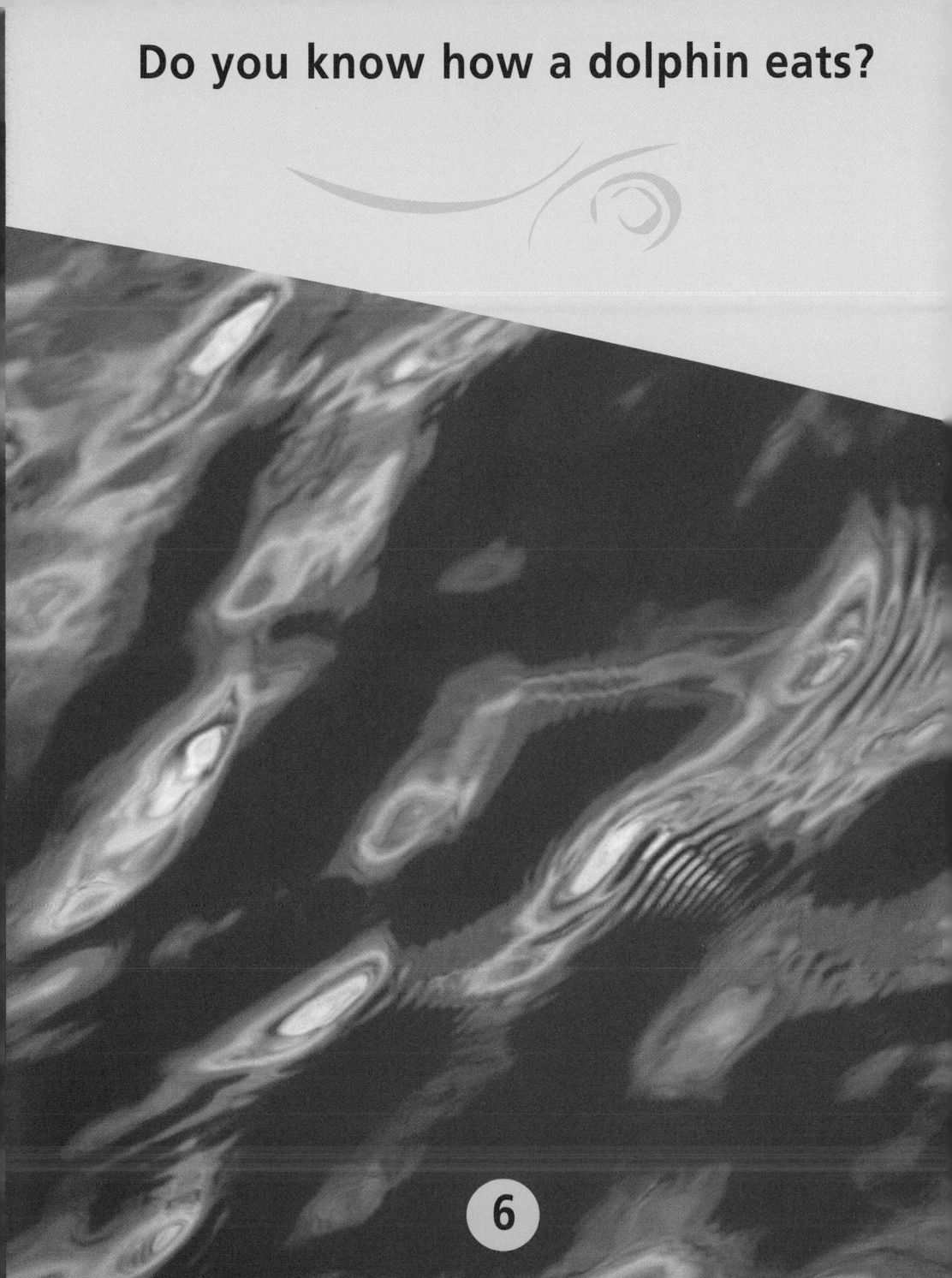

A dolphin breathes
through a hole in its head.
A dolphin comes
above the water to breathe.
It holds its breath
under the water.

Lift the flap
to find out.

Do you know how a dolphin swims fast?

A dolphin has lots of small teeth.
It uses its teeth to hold its food.
A dolphin eats its food whole.

**Lift the flap
to find out.**

Do you know what else a dolphin can do with its tail fin?

A dolphin moves its tail fin
up and down to swim fast.
Its smooth body helps it swim fast.

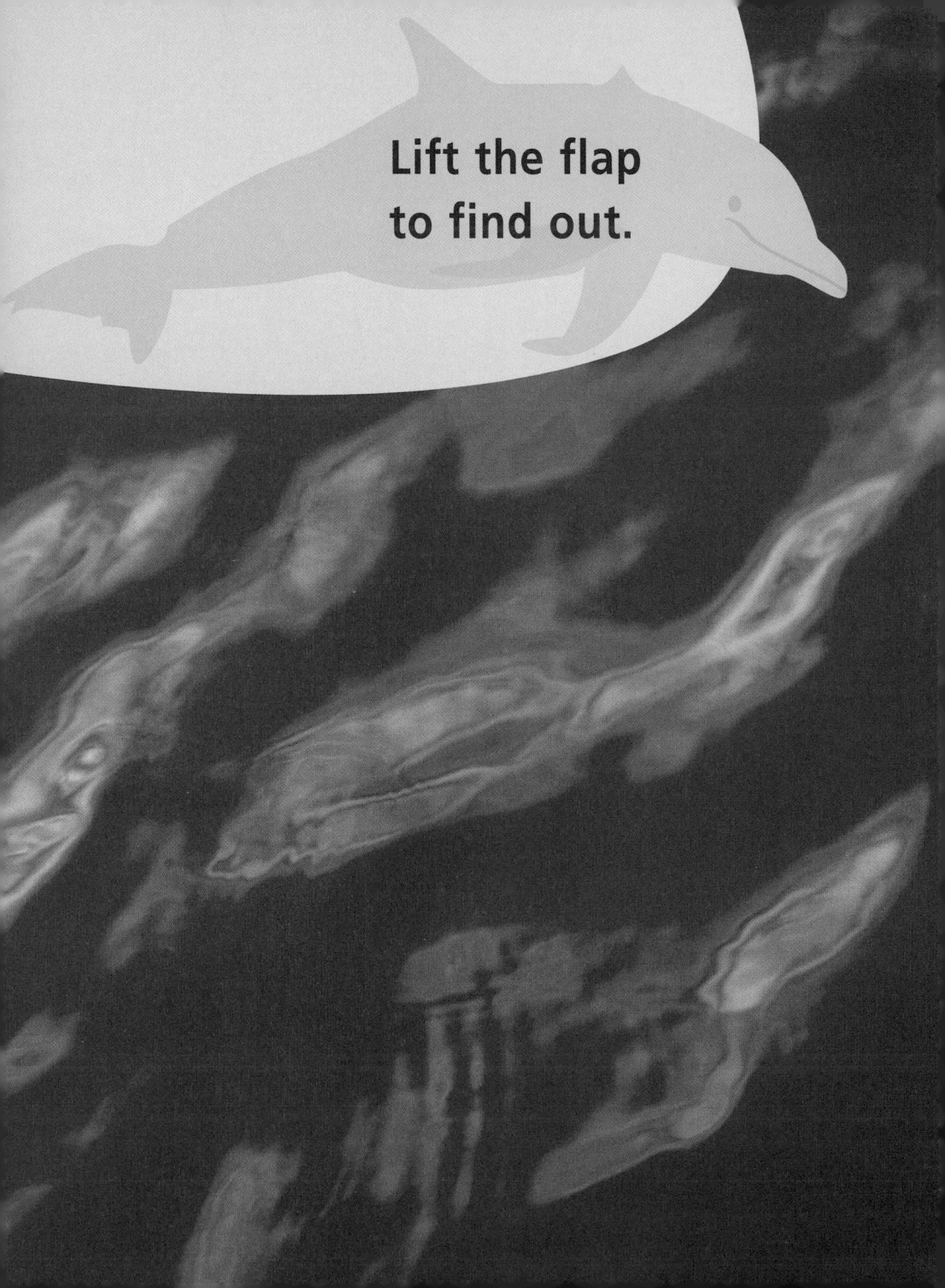

Lift the flap
to find out.

It can stand on its tail fin.

11

Index